THE 'INVISIBLE' ADDER - PAGE 6

AWESOME!

CONTENTS

KT-164-732

THE SUPER SHIELD OF THE HERMIT CRAB - PAGE 22

THE SUPER NATURAL WORLD OF ANIMALS

Welcome to the supernatural world of the animal kingdom. This book will take you on an amazing journey to meet some of the world's weirdest and most wonderful animals. Are you ready for the ride?

Every day we process information from five key senses – sight, hearing, smell, touch, and taste – so that we can make sense of the world and communicate with others. Animals have their own ways of sensing the world. Some have sharper sight, stronger smell, super-sensitive touch, or even senses that are completely outside our own experience – so much so that they appear to be supernatural powers!

SUPER SIGHT

Vision helps animals find food, move around, and hide from predators. Some animals have far sharper eyesight than our own and can see things much more clearly. Others see the world completely differently, sensing forms of light that are invisible to the human eye.

FINELY TUNED

All vertebrates (animals with a backbone) can hear. Some have a remarkable sense of hearing and can detect the faintest of noises.

SMELL & TASTE

A sharp sense of smell helps an animal to find food, pick up the scent of a mate, avoid an enemy or sniff its way through an unfamiliar place.

SUPER NATURAL ANIMALS

AWESOME CREATURES AND THEIR  **SUPER POWERS!**

LEON GRAY

WAYLAND

THE HEAT-SEEKING
SUPERSONIC VAMPIRE
BAT - PAGE 42

THE X-RAY EARS OF THE
FENNEC FOX - PAGE 16

Published in paperback in 2014 by Wayland
Copyright © Wayland 2014

Wayland
338 Euston Road
London NW1 3BH

Wayland Australia
Level 17/207
Kent Street
Sydney, NSW 2000

Editor: Nicola Edwards
Designer: Rocket Design (East Anglia) Ltd

Dewey categorisation: 508

ISBN 978 0 7502 8386 1

Printed in China

10 9 8 7 6 5 4 3 2 1

Wayland is a division of Hachette Children's Books,
an Hachette UK company.
www.hachette.co.uk

Picture acknowledgements:
The author and publisher would like to thank the following
for allowing their pictures to be reproduced in this publication:
Pictures by Shutterstock except for p6 iStock;
p13 B G Thomson/Science Photo Library;
p14 Willem Kolvoort/naturepl.com;
p31Kevin Schafer/naturepl.com;
p39 Guy Edwards/naturepl.com;
p43 Jim Clare/naturepl.com

SKIN DEEP

Some animals are nocturnal, which means they are active at night. Others live in complete darkness all the time – for example, in a cave or under the ground. Good eyesight is useless in the dark, so instead these animals have developed super-sensory touch to feel their way around. Some animals even have special touch organs, such as whiskers, to help them move around in safety.

SUPER NATURAL POWER!

There are some animals that have developed supernatural powers outside our own experience. Can you imagine being able to **see in sound**, detect the body heat of other animals, or pick up the movements of your prey as tiny pulses of electricity? And some animal superpowers are just plain odd – such as the ability to **shape-shift into different forms**, regenerate lost body parts, or **spray a cocktail of toxic chemicals** at an enemy.

LOOK OUT FOR THESE SPECIAL FEATURES!

THE 'INVISIBLE' ADDER

DESPITE ITS BITE THE ADDER IS KNOWN AS THE 'SHY SNAKE'.

The shy, secretive adder is the only British reptile with a deadly venomous bite. Reptiles are cold-blooded creatures and prefer warm places with lots of sunshine. Since the weather in the UK is usually cool and damp, adders hibernate in winter and emerge in the warmer spring to mate.

Living up to its description as the 'shy snake', an adder would prefer to make a speedy escape than get into a fight. Adder bites on humans are rare and usually occur when a person accidentally steps on a snake basking in the sun. Like all snakes in the viper family, the adder's venom is haemotoxic, which means it **poisons the blood**. The venom causes severe pain and can be deadly.

CRITTER STATS!

Size: Up to 80cm
Number of species: 1
Habitat: Woods and wetlands

THE HUMAN FACTOR

SCIENTISTS HAVE USED CARBON NANOTUBES – MOLECULAR SHEETS OF CARBON ROLLED INTO TUBES – TO MAKE A REAL INVISIBILITY CLOAK. THE TECHNOLOGY WORKS IN THE SAME WAY AS A MIRAGE, BENDING LIGHT AROUND THE NANOTUBE SHEET TO MAKE IT INVISIBLE.

SUPER NATURAL POWER!

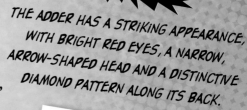

Out in the open, an adder would be easy to spot. But hidden away in its favourite habitat – open woodland, heaths, moors and river banks – the snake's skin colour and markings give it a **near-perfect camouflage**. Not only does the adder's **cloak of invisibility** hide it from misplaced human footsteps, it also serves as an excellent disguise for its favourite prey: mice, voles, birds and frogs.

STRIKE FORCE!

Snakes do not have legs but they can move surprisingly quickly. Adders slither along the ground in a 'serpentine' motion, which means they weave their bodies from side to side. Scales on the adder's belly press against bumps on the ground to move its body forward. But the real surprise is the speed of the adder's strike. An adder can strike and **take out its prey in a fraction of a second,** making it one of the world's fastest and deadliest predators.

AWESOME!

THE ADDER HAS A STRIKING APPEARANCE, WITH BRIGHT RED EYES, A NARROW, ARROW-SHAPED HEAD AND A DISTINCTIVE DIAMOND PATTERN ALONG ITS BACK.

MEANWHILE, AT THE MOVIES...

SUPERHERO STYLE

WELL KNOWN COMIC BOOK CHARACTERS AND ACTION HEROES WHO HAVE INVISIBILITY SUPERPOWERS INCLUDE:

RICK JONES THIS MARVEL UNIVERSE SUPERHERO HAS AN ADDER-LIKE ABILITY TO CAMOUFLAGE HIMSELF. THIS ENABLES HIM TO REMAIN UNDETECTED WHILE HE STALKS HIS ENEMIES.

HARRY POTTER WEARS A MAGICAL CLOAK TO MAKE HIMSELF INVISIBLE, HELPING HIM ON COUNTLESS TRIPS AND MISSIONS AGAINST HIS ARCH-ENEMY LORD VOLDEMORT.

THE CASSOWARY: ARMED AND DANGEROUS

Living deep in the rainforests of Australia and New Guinea, the tall and heavy cassowary bird rarely encounters people and usually makes its escape before it is discovered. Even so, many people consider the cassowary to be one of the most terrifying birds in the world!

The cassowary cannot fly because of its **enormous size and bulk**. Instead, it roams among the dense rainforest vegetation in search of juicy fruits, shoots, insects, and small animals such as mice, frogs and small lizards.

WOW!

THE CASSOWARY IS ONE OF THE WORLD'S BIGGEST BIRDS – ONLY THE OSTRICH AND EMU ARE BIGGER.

CRITTER STATS!

Size: 2m tall; wingspan 2m

Number of species: 3

Habitat: Rainforests

SUPER NATURAL POWER!

The cassowary is armed with a long, sharp claw on each foot. The middle of the three toes has an **enormous dagger-like claw** that can reach up to 12cm in length. Cassowaries use their deadly claws as a form of defence. They kick out with their powerful legs, using their claws to **inflict serious injuries**. These birds can run up to 50km per hour and swim and jump well, so it is difficult to escape from an angry cassowary!

HELMET HEAD

If you were lucky enough to spot a cassowary in the wild, one of the first things you would notice – apart from its huge size – is the bird's **distinctive head**. The cassowary has a large 'helmet', called a casque, on top of its head. No one really knows what purpose the casque serves. Some people think that it protects the bird's head as it speeds through the dense rainforest. Others suggest that the casque plays a part in the cassowary's **booming birdsong,** which helps these giant birds communicate in the rainforest.

AWESOME!

THE CASQUE IS MADE FROM A SUBSTANCE CALLED KERATIN, WHICH IS THE SAME MATERIAL THAT MAKES UP YOUR FINGERNAILS.

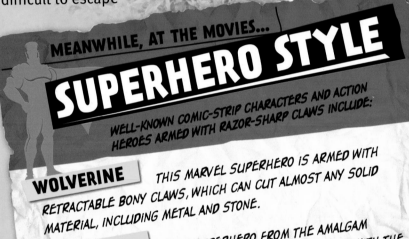

MEANWHILE, AT THE MOVIES...

SUPERHERO STYLE

WELL-KNOWN COMIC-STRIP CHARACTERS AND ACTION HEROES ARMED WITH RAZOR-SHARP CLAWS INCLUDE:

WOLVERINE THIS MARVEL SUPERHERO IS ARMED WITH RETRACTABLE BONY CLAWS, WHICH CAN CUT ALMOST ANY SOLID MATERIAL, INCLUDING METAL AND STONE.

DARK CLAW THIS SUPERHERO FROM THE AMALGAM UNIVERSE COMBINES THE DEADLY CLAWS OF WOLVERINE WITH THE SHARP SENSES AND AMAZING SUPERPOWERS OF BATMAN.

THE CRAZY COLOUR-CHANGING CHAMELEON

CRITTER STATS!

Size: Ranges from 1.5cm to 70cm

Number of species: About 160

Habitat: Mainly trees in forests

There are more than 100 different types of chameleon living in warm places around the world, especially Africa and the island of Madagascar. The most amazing thing about these reptiles is their supernatural colour-changing power. Chameleons use this to hide from their enemies and as a way of communicating with each other.

Chameleons prefer to live in warm places because they are reptiles. These cold-blooded creatures bask in the sun to warm their blood. Only then can they start to roam among the branches of trees in search of food. Chameleons are **specially adapted for life in the treetops.** They have strong toes and sharp claws that help them to grip tightly on the rough bark of narrow branches as they climb.

THE HUMAN FACTOR

WHEN EXPOSED TO SUNLIGHT, YOU MIGHT HAVE NOTICED THAT YOUR SKIN BECOMES DARKER. THIS IS DUE TO A SKIN PIGMENT CALLED MELANIN. IT GROWS DARKER IN STRONG SUNLIGHT TO PROTECT THE SKIN FROM THE DAMAGING EFFECTS OF ULTRAVIOLET RADIATION.

SUPER NATURAL POWER!

Many chameleons change the colour of their scaly skin to match their surroundings and hide from predators such as birds and snakes. The skin of a chameleon contains special cells full of **substances called pigments** that give chameleons their colourful appearance.

As well as camouflage, chameleons change colour to **communicate with each other**. Dark colours usually mean a chameleon is angry, while males turn bright pink, red or turquoise to attract females. Chameleons also change colour to **maintain their body temperature**. Darker colours absorb sunlight to warm the chameleon's skin in the morning. Brighter colours reflect sunlight during the hottest part of the day.

MEANWHILE, AT THE MOVIES...
SUPERHERO STYLE

COLOUR-CHANGING COMIC-STRIP CHARACTERS AND ACTION HEROES INCLUDE:

CHAMELEON AN ARCH-ENEMY OF SPIDER-MAN AND A MASTER OF DISGUISE WHO CHANGES APPEARANCE TO FOOL HIS ENEMIES.

THE COLOR KID THIS DC COMICS SUPERHERO CAN CHANGE THE COLOUR OF ANY OBJECT HE TOUCHES AND SHOOT BEAMS OF COLOURED LIGHT AT HIS OPPONENTS TO BLIND THEM.

FEEDING FRENZY

Most of a chameleon's day is spent foraging for insects. Its bulging eyes can move independently of each other and pick out the movements of tiny bugs. The chameleon then shoots out its long tongue, which sticks to the prey and recoils back into its mouth instantly.

AWESOME!

THE CHAMELEON'S TONGUE IS ALMOST TWICE THE LENGTH OF ITS BODY.

DUCK-BILLED PLATYPUS

CRITTER STATS!

Size: Up to 50cm long
Number of species: 1
Habitat: Rivers and streams

Scientists first discovered the platypus swimming in a river in New South Wales, Australia, in the late 18th century. It had such unusual appearance that they did not think the animal was real. In fact, the strange body of the platypus is well adapted for swimming. It has webbed feet, a rudder-like tail, and waterproof fur. The fur traps a layer of air beside the body of the platypus to keep it warm as it dives under the water to seek out prey. To make matters even more confusing, the platypus is one of only five mammals to reproduce by laying eggs. Most other mammals give birth to live young.

WOW!

THE PLATYPUS IS A UNIQUE CREATURE THAT COMBINES THE BILL AND WEBBED FEET OF A DUCK WITH THE BODY OF AN OTTER AND THE TAIL OF A BEAVER.

SUPER NATURAL POWER!

Duck-billed platypuses live in rivers and streams across eastern Australia. They dive under the water to search for prey. Since the water is so dark and murky, the platypus cannot rely on eyesight to find its prey. In fact, it dives with its eyes closed. Instead, the platypus relies on its **amazing power of electrolocation** to find food. It uses sensitive electroreceptors in its enormous bill to 'see' electricity generated by the moving muscles of prey such as small fish, crustaceans, and aquatic insects, snails and worms.

AWESOME!

THE PLATYPUS USES ITS BILL AS A SHOVEL TO DIG UP FOOD AND GRAVEL FROM THE RIVER BED. AS IT DOES NOT HAVE TEETH, THE PIECES OF GRAVEL HELP THE PLATYPUS TO GRIND UP THE FOOD.

MEANWHILE, AT THE MOVIES...

SUPERHERO STYLE

WELL-KNOWN COMIC-STRIP CHARACTERS AND ANIMATED ACTION HEROES THAT CAN DETECT ELECTRICITY INCLUDE:

ELECTRO AN ARCH-ENEMY OF SPIDER-MAN AND A MASTER OF DISGUISE WHO CHANGES APPEARANCE TO FOOL HIS ENEMIES.

LIVEWIRE THIS DC COMICS SUPERHERO CAN CHANGE THE COLOUR OF ANY OBJECT HE TOUCHES AND SHOOT BEAMS OF COLOURED LIGHT AT HIS OPPONENTS TO BLIND THEM.

POISON SPUR

POISON SPUR

The platypus is even more unusual because it is one of the very few poisonous mammals in the world. The males have a curved 'spur' on their rear legs, which is attached to a venom gland under the skin. The venom is not deadly to people but is thought to be extremely painful. No one really knows why the males have these spurs. One idea is that they use them to fight with other males during the breeding season.

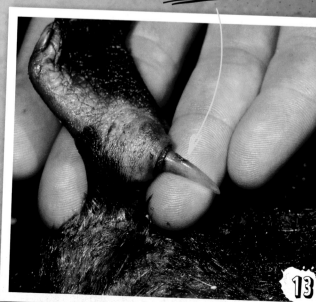

THE ELECTRIC ZAPPING EEL

The electric eel is one of the weirdest fish in the rivers of the Amazon Basin in South America. These huge animals grow up to 2.5 metres long and can weigh up to 20kg. As their name suggests, electric eels use electricity to stun and kill their prey, as well as to defend themselves from any predators brave enough to take them on.

Living in the murky waters of the Amazon and Orinoco rivers, the electric eel is a large, heavy fish. It stays mainly on the riverbeds but rises to the surface to breathe and search for its prey.

CRITTER STATS!

Size: Up to 2.5m long
Number of species: 1
Habitat: Rivers and streams

THE HUMAN FACTOR

IN SOME COUNTRIES, THE POLICE USE TASER GUNS AS A NON-LETHAL WAY OF DEALING WITH VIOLENT SUSPECTS. THE TASER GUN WORKS BY DELIVERING A MASSIVE ELECTRIC SHOCK, WHICH TEMPORARILY PARALYZES THE SUSPECT'S MUSCLES, STUNNING THEM INTO SUBMISSION.

WOW! THE SKIN OF AN ELECTRIC EEL IS RUBBERY AND SHARK-LIKE. IT IS DARK ON THE BACK AND ORANGE OR YELLOW ON THE BELLY.

SUPER NATURAL POWER!

Three special organs in the electric eel's abdomen enable it to deliver a powerful electric shock. Each organ contains **cells called electrocytes,** which are stacked together and produce electricity in a similar way to a battery.

GROWING UP

Electric eels breed in an unusual way. The male eels build a nest using saliva (spit), and the females lay thousands of eggs in it. These eggs hatch in batches, and **wave after wave of young eels emerge** from the nest. The first-born eels gobble up other eggs and younger hatchlings, before moving on to larger prey such as crabs and shrimp. Adult electric eels usually hunt other fish, but may also eat small mammals and animals as large as caimans (reptiles in the alligator family).

AWESOME!

THE EEL CAN GENERATE AN ELECTRICAL CHARGE OF UP TO 500 VOLTS. THIS WOULD BE POWERFUL ENOUGH TO KILL AN ADULT HUMAN.

MEANWHILE, AT THE MOVIES...

SUPERHERO STYLE

MANY DIFFERENT COMIC-STRIP CHARACTERS AND ACTION HEROES USE ELECTRICITY AS A WEAPON, INCLUDING:

BLACK LIGHTNING THIS SUPERHERO WAS BORN WITH THE ABILITY TO STUN AND KILL HIS ADVERSARIES WITH POWERFUL ELECTRIC SHOCKS. BLACK LIGHTNING ALSO SAVED SUPERMAN'S LIFE WITH AN ELECTRIC SHOCK THAT RESTARTED HIS HEART.

SURGE A FEMALE SUPERHERO WHO CAN ABSORB ELECTRICITY FROM THE AIR AND THEN DISCHARGE IT AS POWERFUL BOLTS OF LIGHTNING. SHE ALSO CHANNELS THE ELECTRICAL ENERGY INTO BURSTS OF SUPERHUMAN SPEED.

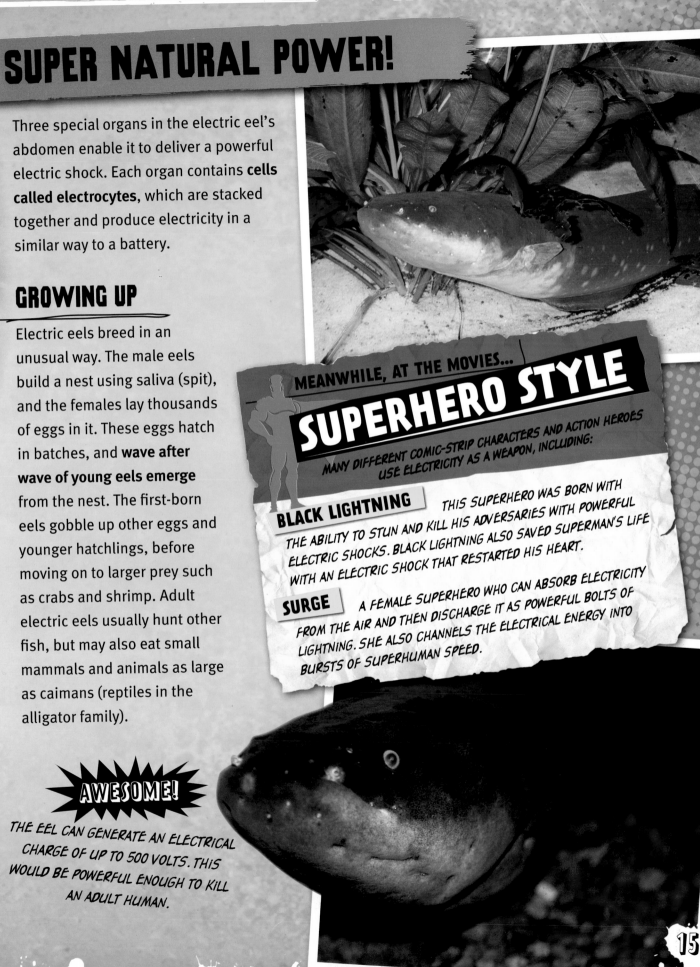

THE X-RAY EARS OF THE FENNEC FOX

Fennec foxes are small mammals that live in the Sahara Desert in North Africa. This small nocturnal predator stays in an underground den during the hottest part of the day and emerges at dusk to hunt. It has two enormous ears and super-sensitive hearing to pick up the slightest movement of prey such as insects, birds, rodents, and rabbits.

These foxes are well adapted for life in the scorching desert. Their large ears help to radiate heat away from the body to keep cool, and their creamy-coloured fur reflects the bright sunlight. Fennec foxes can also survive without much water. In fact, they get most of their water from their food. The fox's kidneys reabsorb most of the moisture from its food back into the body to prevent losing too much water.

CRITTER STATS!

Size: Around 70cm from head to tail

Number of species: 1

Habitat: Sahara Desert

THICK FUR COVERS THE FOX'S PAWS TO STOP IT BURNING ITS FEET ON THE HOT SAND.

SUPER NATURAL POWER!

A fennec fox has a supernatural sense of hearing. Its ears are huge in relation to the size of its body. Each ear measures 15 cm (6 inches) long, which is half the size of the entire body. Fennec foxes use their enormous ears to locate the movement of prey such as rabbits and rodents, which burrow under the ground. They can also detect the faintest sound of a cricket tiptoeing across the desert sand.

FRIENDLY FOXES

Fennec foxes are social animals that live in family groups. A male and female fox usually pair up for life and rear their young in an underground den. The young foxes learn all their hunting skills by playing with each other. Even the adult foxes join in a game of rough and tumble!

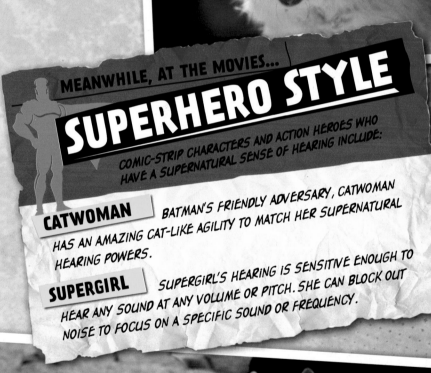

MEANWHILE, AT THE MOVIES...
SUPERHERO STYLE

COMIC-STRIP CHARACTERS AND ACTION HEROES WHO HAVE A SUPERNATURAL SENSE OF HEARING INCLUDE:

CATWOMAN BATMAN'S FRIENDLY ADVERSARY, CATWOMAN HAS AN AMAZING CAT-LIKE AGILITY TO MATCH HER SUPERNATURAL HEARING POWERS.

SUPERGIRL SUPERGIRL'S HEARING IS SENSITIVE ENOUGH TO HEAR ANY SOUND AT ANY VOLUME OR PITCH. SHE CAN BLOCK OUT NOISE TO FOCUS ON A SPECIFIC SOUND OR FREQUENCY.

AWESOME!

YOUNG FENNEC FOXES STAY WITH THEIR PARENTS EVEN AFTER A NEW LITTER OF BABY FOXES IS BORN.

THE ANTI-GRAVITY GECKO

- Geckos belong to a large group of lizards that live in warm places around the world. There are more than 1,500 different species, and many of them are very colourful reptiles. Almost all geckos have excellent eyesight. But perhaps the most amazing thing about them is their ability to climb up surfaces as smooth as glass.

These lizards live in many different places, from the deserts of southwestern USA to the rainforests of Southeast Asia. Unlike most reptiles, which bask in the heat of the sun to warm up their cold blood, many geckos are **active at night**. They use their **supernatural sense of eyesight** to spot prey in the darkness. In fact, a gecko's night vision is more than 350 times more sensitive than our own eyesight.

CRITTER STATS!

Size: Ranges from 1 to 60 cm

Number of species: More than 1,500

Habitat: Ranges from deserts and forests to people's homes

SUPER NATURAL POWER!

Geckos are fantastic climbers. These reptiles have **special glue-grip feet** that allow them to climb up almost any surface. Each footpad is covered with thousands of **hair-like structures called setae**. Every square millimetre of the footpad has around 14,000 setae, providing a huge surface area to cling to surfaces. The setae are tipped with even smaller structures called spatulae. The setae and spatulae combine to exert a **powerful adhesive force**.

AWESOME!

THE GECKO CAN CLIMB UP ALMOST ANY SURFACE - EVEN WHEN IT IS UPSIDE DOWN!

LOSING LIMBS

Another unusual behaviour of the gecko is its ability to **shed its tail** when predators such as birds and snakes attack. After the gecko loses its limb, the detached tail continues to wriggle around on the floor. This confuses the predator so the gecko can make good its escape.

THE HUMAN FACTOR

SCIENTISTS ARE INVENTING MATERIALS THAT COPY THE AMAZING ANTIGRAVITY GLUE-GRIP FEET OF GECKOS. THEY HAVE DEVELOPED MICROSCOPIC CARBON NANOTUBES - MOLECULAR SHEETS OF CARBON ROLLED INTO TUBES. THE NANOTUBES ACT LIKE THE HAIR-LIKE SETAE ON A GECKO'S FOOT.

MEANWHILE, AT THE MOVIES...

SUPERHERO STYLE

MANY DIFFERENT COMIC-STRIP CHARACTERS AND ACTION HEROES CAN MATCH THE AMAZING CLIMBING ABILITY OF THE GECKO, INCLUDING:

NIGHTCRAWLER

THIS SUPERHERO HAS AMAZING AGILITY AND CLINGS TO SURFACES USING MICROSCOPIC SUCTION CUPS ATTACHED TO HIS HANDS AND FEET.

SPIDER-MAN

SPIDER-MAN IS FAMOUS FOR HIS WALL-CRAWLING ABILITY, STICKING TO SEEMINGLY IMPOSSIBLE SURFACES, SUCH AS GLASS, USING ONLY HIS HANDS AND FEET.

THE SUPER-SENSORY GIANT ANTEATER

Giant anteaters are insect-eating animals that live in the grasslands and forests of Central and South America. These large mammals have an unusually long snout and an incredible sense of smell, which they use to sniff out their favourite food: ants and termites.

In one day, a giant anteater can gobble up 30,000 ants or termites, tearing open anthills and termite mounds with their powerful claws. They also eat beetle and honeybee larvae, which are often found inside the muddy mounds. Occasionally, an anteater will eat fruit.

As the giant anteater has no teeth, it uses its enormous tongue to lap up and swallow its food. The tongue is very sticky and very long – stretching out up to 50 cm. The tongue moves in and out of the mouth rapidly when the anteater feeds – up to 160 times every minute.

CRITTER STATS!

Size: Up to 2m long
Number of species: 1
Habitat: Forests, grasslands and swamps

WOW!

THE ANTEATER'S SNOUT IS ACTUALLY A LONG JAW THAT ENDS WITH A SMALL, MOIST NOSE.

SUPER NATURAL POWER!

Anteaters do not have very good hearing or eyesight but use their long snouts and **supernatural sense of smell** to locate their food. So powerful is its sense of smell that it can detect ants and termites from many kilometres away.

FIGHTING BACK

Anteaters eat their prey so quickly because the ants and termites possess a painful sting. The anteater **relies on surprise** to raid anthills and termite mounds. It then feasts on as many insects as possible before the insects rally together and fight back. The anteater will then retreat, leaving the nest intact as a future source of food.

AWESOME!

THE GIANT ANTEATER'S SENSE OF SMELL IS UP TO 40 TIMES MORE POWERFUL THAN OUR OWN.

MEANWHILE, AT THE MOVIES...

SUPERHERO STYLE

SOME COMIC-STRIP CHARACTERS AND ACTION HEROES WITH A SUPERNATURAL SENSE OF SMELL INCLUDE:

BLADE THIS SUPERHERO VAMPIRE HUNTER RELIES ON HIS KEEN SENSE OF SMELL TO SNIFF OUT SUPERNATURAL CREATURES.

THE BLACK PANTHER THIS COMIC-BOOK HERO HAS A SUPERHUMAN SENSE OF SMELL AND CAN REMEMBER TENS OF THOUSANDS OF INDIVIDUAL SCENTS.

THE SUPER SHIELD OF THE HERMIT CRAB

WOW!

THERE ARE MORE THAN 1,100 DIFFERENT TYPES OF HERMIT CRAB.

Hermit crabs belong to a large group of animals called crustaceans. Most crustaceans have a hard outer shell, called an exoskeleton, to protect their soft bodies. Hermit crabs do not have an exoskeleton. Instead, they use the cast-off shells of other creatures for protection.

Some hermit crabs live on the seashore, hiding among rockpools, while others live in the deep ocean. A few hermit crabs are even found living on the land – such as the giant coconut crab, which measures more than 2 metres long and is the world's biggest hermit crab.

THE HUMAN FACTOR

IN THE 1960S, SCIENTISTS DEVELOPED BULLETPROOF BODY ARMOUR FOR USE IN WARFARE AND CRIME FIGHTING. UNLIKE TRADITIONAL ARMOUR, MODERN BODY ARMOUR IS SOFT. IT IS MADE FROM ADVANCED FIBRES THAT CAN BE SEWN INTO VESTS AND OTHER PROTECTIVE CLOTHING. THE FIBRES ARE WOVEN INTO A STRONG NET THAT DISPERSES THE ENERGY OF THE BULLET TO PREVENT INJURY.

CRITTER STATS!

Size: Up to 2m long

Number of species: About 1,100

Habitat: Mostly in coastal regions and deep oceans

SUPER NATURAL POWER!

Unlike other crustaceans, the body of the hermit crab is unusually soft and in need of protection. Hermit crabs wear the discarded shells of other animals, such as sea snails, as a **suit of body armour**. The hard shell protects hermit crabs from predators, such as cuttlefish, octopuses, sharks, and squid. Sometimes other animals, such as sea anemones, hitch a ride on the hermit crab's adopted shell. This **camouflages the crab** and provides it with even more protection.

SHELL SWAP

As hermit crabs grow in size, they need to find new shells. Sometimes crabs **form queues for the shells**, with the biggest crab leaving its shell behind for a slightly smaller crab, which leaves its own shell for the next smallest crab. Hermit crabs also **compete for the best shells**, ganging up on a crab with a better shell to steal it.

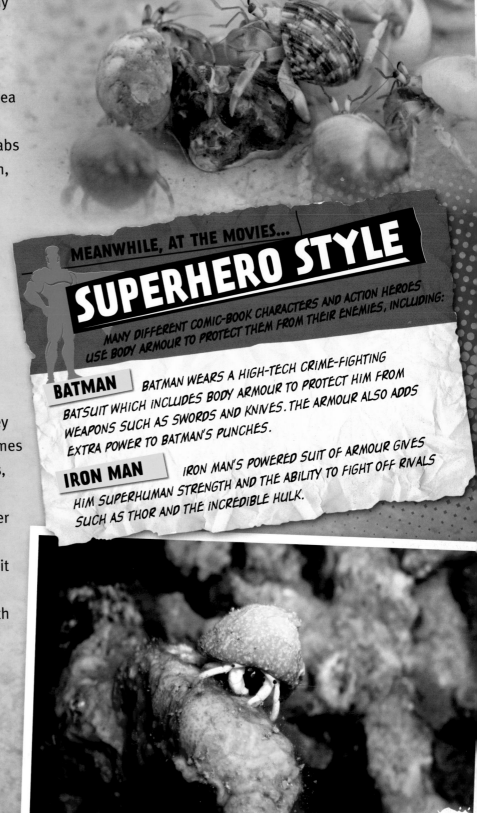

AWESOME!

A HERMIT CRAB'S BODY IS SUPPLE, SO IT CAN TWIST AND SQUEEZE INSIDE ITS NEW HOME.

MEANWHILE, AT THE MOVIES...

SUPERHERO STYLE

MANY DIFFERENT COMIC-BOOK CHARACTERS AND ACTION HEROES USE BODY ARMOUR TO PROTECT THEM FROM THEIR ENEMIES, INCLUDING:

BATMAN BATMAN WEARS A HIGH-TECH CRIME-FIGHTING BATSUIT WHICH INCLUDES BODY ARMOUR TO PROTECT HIM FROM WEAPONS SUCH AS SWORDS AND KNIVES. THE ARMOUR ALSO ADDS EXTRA POWER TO BATMAN'S PUNCHES.

IRON MAN IRON MAN'S POWERED SUIT OF ARMOUR GIVES HIM SUPERHUMAN STRENGTH AND THE ABILITY TO FIGHT OFF RIVALS SUCH AS THOR AND THE INCREDIBLE HULK.

THE SUPER-SPEEDY HUMMINGBIRD

There are more than 320 different hummingbirds, and they are some of the smallest birds on the planet. Indeed, the world's smallest hummingbird is the aptly named bee hummingbird, which measures just 5 cm long.

Most hummingbirds live in the tropical rainforests of Central and South America. A few species live in cooler, temperate parts of North America, and one small group, called the hillstars, live high in the Andes Mountains, more than 5,000 metres above sea level. Hummingbirds come in many different colours and often glisten as they fly. This is called iridescence and is due to the way light bounces off their feathers.

WOW!

HUMMINGBIRDS TAKE THEIR NAME FROM THE SOUND THEIR WINGS MAKE AS THEY HOVER IN THE AIR.

CRITTER STATS!

Size: 5-20cm
Number of species: More than 320
Habitat: Mainly tropical forests

SUPER NATURAL POWER!

No matter what colour they are or where they live, hummingbirds are masters of flight. These super speedy birds beat their wings **up to 80 times per second**, hovering midair as they feed on plant nectar, the sugary liquid found inside the flowers of plants. They have long, curved beaks to probe inside the flowers for their food. During flight, a hummingbird's heart can beat at more than 1,250 times every second.

AWESOME!

HUMMINGBIRDS ARE THE ONLY BIRDS THAT CAN FLY BACKWARDS.

FUEL FOR FLIGHT

Hummingbirds need to feed on a lot of plant nectar to get enough energy to beat their wings so quickly. They top up their diet with insects and spiders, which they hunt on the wing.

Many hummingbirds go into a sleep-like state, called torpor, when they are asleep or when food is scarce. This slows down the birds' high metabolism **to a fraction of its normal state**, which helps to save energy.

SOME SPECIES OF HUMMINGBIRD CONSUME MORE THAN THEIR OWN BODYWEIGHT OF NECTAR EVERY DAY.

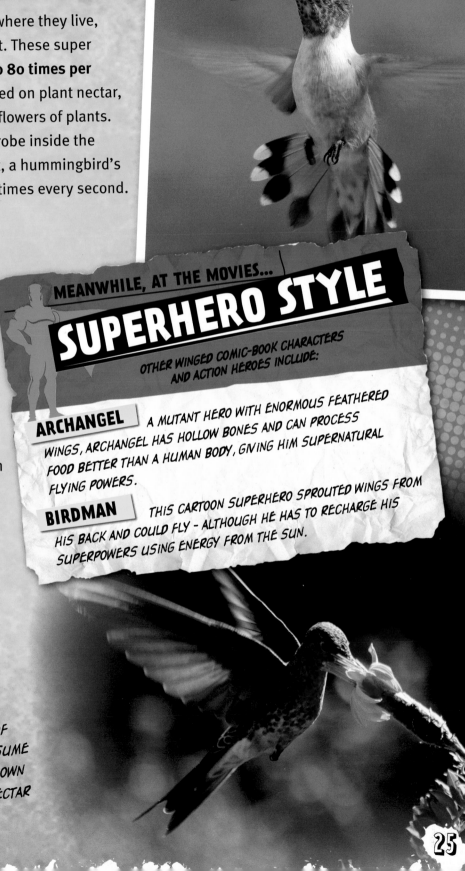

MEANWHILE, AT THE MOVIES...
SUPERHERO STYLE

OTHER WINGED COMIC-BOOK CHARACTERS AND ACTION HEROES INCLUDE:

ARCHANGEL A MUTANT HERO WITH ENORMOUS FEATHERED WINGS, ARCHANGEL HAS HOLLOW BONES AND CAN PROCESS FOOD BETTER THAN A HUMAN BODY, GIVING HIM SUPERNATURAL FLYING POWERS.

BIRDMAN THIS CARTOON SUPERHERO SPROUTED WINGS FROM HIS BACK AND COULD FLY - ALTHOUGH HE HAS TO RECHARGE HIS SUPERPOWERS USING ENERGY FROM THE SUN.

THE BIONIC NEWT

CRITTER STATS!

Size: Up to 15cm

Number of species: About 40

Habitat: Wetlands

Newts are amphibians that look like a cross between a lizard and a frog. Like frogs, they start their lives as tadpoles. As they grow, they undergo a series of changes called metamorphosis before reaching their lizard-like adult form. One of the main supernatural powers of newts is their bionic bodies.

When adult newts are ready to mate, the females lay single eggs in the water and the males fertilize them. The eggs then hatch into tadpoles with feathery external gills. Over several months, the tadpoles grow legs and lungs to breathe air and move onto the land. The newt is then known as an eft. The eft develops into an adult newt, which may stay on the land or return to the water.

THE HUMAN FACTOR

SCIENTISTS ARE INTERESTED IN THE REGENERATIVE POWER OF NEWTS. THEY HOPE TO COPY THIS SUPERNATURAL ABILITY TO REGENERATE LIMBS IN HUMAN PATIENTS.

AWESOME!

AS AQUATIC ANIMALS, NEWTS SPEND THEIR TIME IN OR NEAR WATER, AND RETURN TO THE WATER TO BREED.

SUPER NATURAL POWER!

One of the most amazing things about newts is their ability to **grow back lost limbs** and other body parts. This process is called regeneration, and it is especially useful when predators attack and injure the newt's body, for example, when it loses a tail.

AWESOME!

REGENERATION WORKS BECAUSE CELLS AT THE SITE OF THE INJURY CAN DIVIDE AND GROW QUICKLY TO MAKE NEW BODY PARTS.

TOXIC NEWTS

The striking orange, yellow or red skin colours of many newts warn potential predators that the **creatures are toxic**. The moist skin of the newt secretes the toxic substance, which then **poisons the predator**. The rough-skinned newt is particularly toxic and produces enough toxin to kill an adult human.

MEANWHILE, AT THE MOVIES...
SUPERHERO STYLE

MANY DIFFERENT COMIC-BOOK CHARACTERS AND SUPERHEROES HAVE THE ABILITY TO REGENERATE BODY PARTS, INCLUDING:

THE INCREDIBLE HULK THE HULK HAS AMAZING HEALING AND REGENERATIVE POWERS. HE CAN GROW NEW TISSUE TO HELP HIM BREATHE IN SPACE AND UNDERWATER. HIS BODY CAN HEAL MOST WOUNDS WITHIN SECONDS.

WOLVERINE WOLVERINE CAN REGENERATE ALMOST EVERY DAMAGED BODY PART. IN FACT, THIS SUPERHERO IS VIRTUALLY INDESTRUCTIBLE, HAVING SURVIVED A NUCLEAR EXPLOSION!

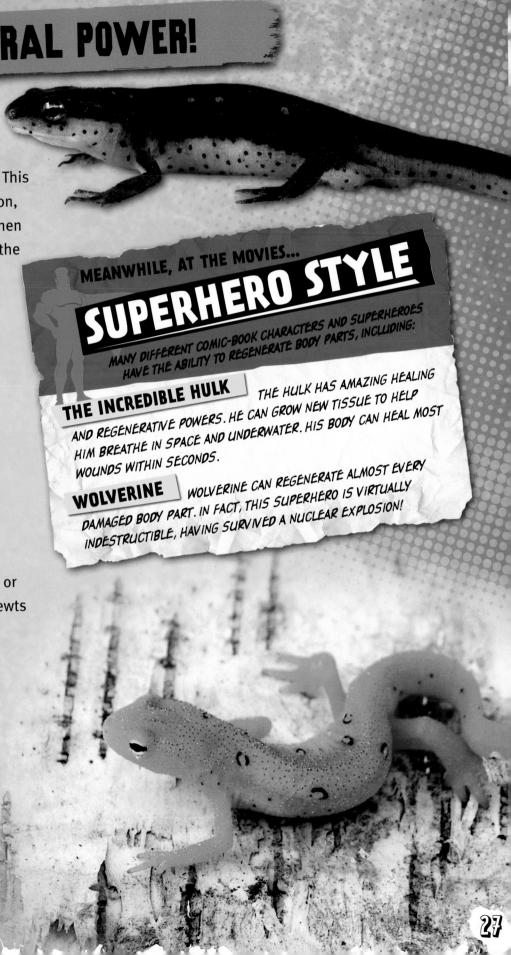

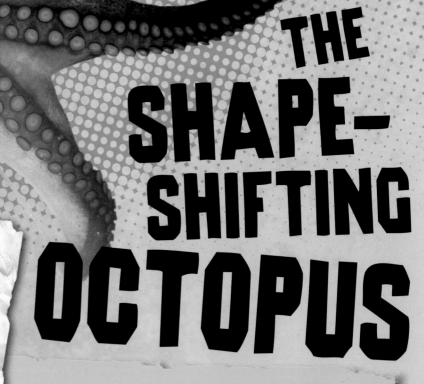

THE SHAPE-SHIFTING OCTOPUS

CRITTER STATS!

Size:
1cm – more than 5m

Number of species:
About 300

Habitat: Tropical and temperate oceans

WOW!

AN OCTOPUS CAN SQUEEZE ITSELF INTO IMPOSSIBLY SMALL SPACES TO ESCAPE FROM PREDATORS.

The octopus takes its name from its eight flexible arms. It 'tastes' its food using the super-sensitive suction cups that cover its arms. These marine animals have amazing powers of regeneration, so if they lose an arm, another grows back in its place!

Octopuses have two bulging eyes and excellent eyesight. They hunt by stalking their prey from above and then sinking down and enveloping the unfortunate victim in their net-like bodies. Some octopuses inject a poison into their prey to paralyse them. This poison is so potent that it can kill a person within 15 minutes.

Octopuses are invertebrates, which means they do not have a bony skeleton inside their bodies. In fact, they have completely soft bodies, which gives the octopus its amazing shape-shifting superpowers.

The octopus uses another superpower to escape predators. When threatened, it squirts a jet of dark blue-black ink from a sac inside its mantle (body). It uses jet-powered propulsion to make a speedy escape, sucking seawater into its mantle and then squirting a jet of water back out.

AWESOME!

THE DARK CLOUD OF INK CONFUSES THE PREDATOR, GIVING THE OCTOPUS TIME TO MAKE ITS ESCAPE.

MASTERS OF DISGUISE

Octopuses have yet another defence against predators. They can change the colour and texture of their skin to act as camouflage. The body of the octopus contains sacs of pigment that change colour when the animal squeezes or relaxes the muscles in its skin. The same muscles can also transform the texture of the octopus's skin to look like a craggy coral reef or sandy sea floor.

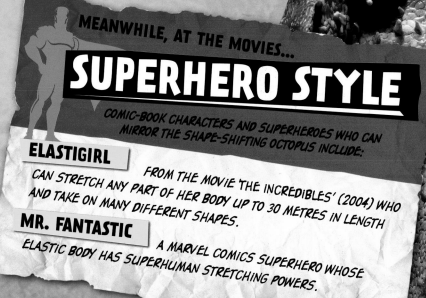

MEANWHILE, AT THE MOVIES...

SUPERHERO STYLE

COMIC-BOOK CHARACTERS AND SUPERHEROES WHO CAN MIRROR THE SHAPE-SHIFTING OCTOPUS INCLUDE:

ELASTIGIRL
FROM THE MOVIE 'THE INCREDIBLES' (2004) WHO CAN STRETCH ANY PART OF HER BODY UP TO 30 METRES IN LENGTH AND TAKE ON MANY DIFFERENT SHAPES.

MR. FANTASTIC
A MARVEL COMICS SUPERHERO WHOSE ELASTIC BODY HAS SUPERHUMAN STRETCHING POWERS.

THE SUPERSONIC PINK RIVER DOLPHIN

CRITTER STATS!

Size: Up to 3m

Number of species: 1

Habitat: Amazon and Orinoco rivers

WOW!

THE BRAIN OF AN ADULT DOLPHIN IS 40 PER CENT BIGGER THAN A HUMAN BRAIN COMPARED TO THE SIZE OF ITS BODY.

Pink river dolphins are freshwater mammals that live in the Amazon and Orinoco river basins of South America. These colourful creatures rely on their supersonic sense of hearing to hunt the many different types of fish that swim in the murky waters.

Pink river dolphins are intelligent, curious and playful animals. The Amazonian people that live by the rivers worship the dolphins, believing them to have magical powers. Once a common sight in the rivers of South America, the pink river dolphin is now facing extinction as people pollute the rivers and destroy the surrounding rainforests.

SUPER NATURAL POWER!

Pink river dolphins rely on a **supersonic sense of hearing** to catch fish, their main source of food. These dolphins send out **high-frequency sound waves** from the top of their heads. When the sound waves hit the fish, the dolphin pinpoints the location of its prey from the echoes that bounce back towards it.

AWESOME!

THE DOLPHIN SENSES THE ECHOES USING ITS EXTREMELY LONG SNOUT, WHICH ACTS LIKE AN ANTENNA FOR SOUND WAVES.

SUPERB SWIMMERS

Unlike most other dolphins, pink river dolphins often hunt alone. Since they have few predators there is no need to find safety in numbers. Caimans and alligators rarely attack these dolphins, and human activities pose the only real threat. Pink river dolphins do occasionally hunt in groups, herding fish with gray dolphins that live in the same river. Pink river dolphins are much slower than dolphins that live in the open ocean, but they are still excellent swimmers due to their rubbery paddle-like flippers.

MEANWHILE, AT THE MOVIES...
SUPERHERO STYLE

COMIC-BOOK CHARACTERS AND SUPERHEROES THAT HAVE SUPERSONIC SENSES INCLUDE:

AQUAMAN THIS DC COMICS SUPERHERO RELIES ON HIS SUPERSONIC SENSES TO 'SEE' IN THE DARK OCEAN DEPTHS.

DAREDEVIL HIS AMAZING SENSE OF HEARING CAN DETECT THE FAINTEST HEARTBEAT FROM GREAT DISTANCES. DAREDEVIL ALSO USES HIS SUPERSONIC HEARING AS A FORM OF RADAR NAVIGATION.

THE HEAT-SEEKING PIT VIPER

Pit vipers are a small group of venomous snakes that take their name from the supersensory pits found between the eye and the nostril on each side of the head. These deep pits can sense the body heat of the vipers' prey, giving these snakes superb night vision.

There are about 150 species of pit viper found in Asia and the Americas. They range in size from the hump-nosed viper, which is about 30 cm long to the formidable bushmaster, which can reach up to 3.6 m in length and is the longest venomous snake in the Americas. This group of venomous snakes also includes the familiar North American rattlesnakes.

CRITTER STATS!

Size: 30cm to 3.6m long

Number of species: About 150

Habitat: Deserts to tropical rainforests

SUPER NATURAL POWER!

The animal equivalent of heat-seeking guidance missiles, these deadly predators can see the body heat of their prey using a special pit organ on each side of the head. The sensory pit, called a fossa, is a complex system of tubes packed with nerve endings. The super-sensitive nerve network can detect infrared radiation, which prey animals give off as body heat.

SENSORY PIT

AWESOME!

THE SENSORY PITS ALLOW THE PIT VIPER TO PINPOINT THE SIZE AND LOCATION OF ITS PREY WITH DEADLY ACCURACY.

NIGHT VISION

Pit vipers are ambush predators. Most species hunt at night, when their supernatural heat-seeking senses come into their own. These ambush predators lie in wait for their favourite prey – rodents and other small mammals – to wander past. Pit vipers strike with incredible speed to deliver their deadly venomous bite. In some cases, the snakes release their prey and wait for the poison to take effect. They use their heat sensors to follow the dying animal until it stops, before swallowing it whole.

MEANWHILE, AT THE MOVIES...
SUPERHERO STYLE

SOME COMIC-BOOK CHARACTERS AND SUPERHEROES THAT CAN DETECT THE INFRARED RADIATION OF OTHER LIVING THINGS INCLUDE:

BLACK CAT MARVEL SUPERHERO BLACK CAT RELIED ON SUPERHUMAN INFRARED NIGHT VISION TO DETECT HER ENEMIES, AND SHE ALSO WORE SPECIAL CONTACT LENSES TO DETECT ULTRAVIOLET LIGHT.

DARKHAWK ANOTHER MARVEL SUPERHERO WITH INFRARED VISION, DARKHAWK COULD EVEN FIRE HEAT BEAMS FROM HIS EYES!

THE POISONOUS SHAPE-SHIFTING PUFFERFISH

Most of the 120 species of fish in the pufferfish group are found in shallow coastal waters in tropical regions around the world, although a few spend all their lives in freshwater. Pufferfish go by many different common names, including balloonfish, blowfish and bubblefish.

The common name of pufferfish refers to their unusual shape-shifting powers. When they are threatened, these fish 'puff up' their bodies to make them look bigger than they actually are. Pufferfish are agile but slow swimmers, so the ability to puff up the body is an essential defence tactic. The pufferfish achieves this shape-shifting feat by filling up its stomach with water. As the fish inflates, spines protrude from its skin, leaving predators faced with an impenetrable spiky ball.

CRITTER STATS!

Size: Up to 1m long

Number of species: At least 120

Habitat: Mainly tropical waters

SUPER NATURAL POWER!

Usually this shape-shifting tactic is enough to scare away most predators. Particularly persistent predators that manage to eat the spiny fish will then face the third (and most lethal) line of protection – the fish's powerful poison.

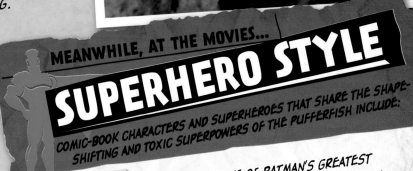

AWESOME!

PUFFERFISH ARE CONSIDERED TO BE THE WORLD'S SECOND MOST POISONOUS VERTEBRATE, AFTER THE GOLDEN POISON FROG.

The poison of the pufferfish is called tetradoxin, and it paralyzes the victim's muscles including the diaphragm, which means most slowly suffocate to death. Many pufferfish have bright colours and striking patterns on their bodies. These distinctive markings warn predators that pufferfish are toxic and definitely not to be messed with!

MEANWHILE, AT THE MOVIES...
SUPERHERO STYLE

COMIC-BOOK CHARACTERS AND SUPERHEROES THAT SHARE THE SHAPE-SHIFTING AND TOXIC SUPERPOWERS OF THE PUFFERFISH INCLUDE:

THE JOKER THE JOKER IS ONE OF BATMAN'S GREATEST ENEMIES AND ONE OF THE FEW SUPER-VILLAINS TO USE POISON, CALLED JOKER VENOM, TO POISON HIS OPPONENTS.

VENOM VENOM IS A PARASITIC VILLAIN WITH SHAPE-SHIFTING POWERS, INCLUDING THE ABILITY TO FORM SPIKES AND PUFF UP ITS BODY.

FOOD FOR THOUGHT

The meat of the pufferfish is a delicacy in Japan, where it is known as fugu. Only licensed chefs can prepare the fugu for consumption because the poison is so lethal. Most people who die from pufferfish poisoning have eaten badly prepared meat.

WOW! A FUGU RESTAURANT IN JAPAN ADVERTISES ITS POTENTIALLY DEADLY DINNERS.

THE TOUCHY-FEELY RACCOON

The raccoon is a common mammal that lives in Central and North America. These furry creatures have also been introduced to other parts of the world, such as Japan and Europe. Raccoons emerge at night to forage for a range of food, from fruits and grubs to small animals such as frogs and mice. What makes these animals so special is their supernatural sense of touch.

Raccoons live in many different habitats – originally forests but now coastal marshes, mountain slopes, and even busy city centres. One of the most striking things about the raccoon is the distinctive black and white bands of fur around the eyes. This bold pattern is called the 'bandit's mask'. Raccoons certainly live up to their notorious reputation. These pesky pests raid rubbish bins at night in search of scraps of food.

CRITTER STATS!

Size: Up to 70cm long (not including tail)

Number of species: 1

Habitat: From marshy forests to busy towns

THE HUMAN FACTOR

RACCOONS ARE CLEVER ANIMALS. ONE OF THE MOST AMAZING SCIENTIFIC STUDIES TOOK PLACE IN 1908, WHEN RACCOONS WERE FOUND TO BE THE ANIMAL EQUIVALENT OF A SAFE CRACKER. THE STUDY SHOWED THAT RACCOONS COULD OPEN COMPLEX LOCKS - EVEN WHEN THE LOCK WAS UPSIDE DOWN!

SUPER NATURAL POWER!

The raccoon's remarkable superpower is its amazing sense of touch. The front paws of these curious creatures are covered with a thin, horny layer that becomes soft when it gets wet. The raccoon then uses super-sensitive structures called vibrissae, just above their sharp claws, to grasp and identify objects at night, when these animals are most active. The sense of touch is further heightened by the unique structure of the raccoon's brain. More than 60 per cent of the brain consists of the cerebral cortex, which is devoted to processing information from the senses.

SUPER SENSES

Equipped with a range of super senses, as well as touch, raccoons have superb night vision. This is thanks to a membrane, called the tapetum lucidum, which captures as much light as possible in the darkness. Raccoons also have a keen sense of smell and fantastic hearing, which is sensitive enough to hear an earthworm burrowing under the ground.

MEANWHILE, AT THE MOVIES...
SUPERHERO STYLE

SOME COMIC-BOOK CHARACTERS AND ACTION HEROES WITH A SUPER SENSE OF TOUCH INCLUDE:

DAREDEVIL DAREDEVIL'S AMAZING TOUCH SENSE IS SO GOOD THAT HE CAN DETECT THE FAINT INK IMPRESSIONS ON A SHEET OF PAPER, ALLOWING HIM TO READ BY TOUCH ALONE.

ROGUE THIS MUTANT SUPERHERO CAN ABSORB THE MEMORIES AND SUPERPOWERS OF ANYTHING SHE TOUCHES!

AWESOME!

YOU CAN SEE THE TAPETUM LUCIDUM GLOW IF YOU SHINE A TORCH AT A RACCOON AT NIGHT.

THE SPITTING COBRA'S TOXIC SPRAY

A small group of snakes, spitting cobras attack their enemies in an unusual way. These deadly spitting snakes do not immediately bite to inject their venom. First, they shoot a spray of lethal venom from their fangs at the eyes of their attackers. Then, if this does not deter the attack, the cobra strikes with a lethal bite – time and time again.

There are 12 species of spitting cobra that slither around the deserts and dry grasslands of Africa and Asia. These deadly snakes come in many different colours and sizes. They hunt an equally varied range of animals, including birds, frogs, lizards and other snakes. The largest species is the brown spitting cobra, which measures up to 2.5 metres long. This species lives in the African savannah and has the deadliest venom of all the spitting cobras.

CRITTER STATS!

Size: Up to 2.5m long
Number of species: 12
Habitat: Deserts and grasslands

ONE BITE FROM A BROWN SPITTING COBRA HAS ENOUGH VENOM TO KILL UP TO 20 PEOPLE!

SUPER NATURAL POWER!

The spitting cobra's venomous spray defends the snake against attackers. When a spitting cobra feels threatened, it rears up off the ground, hisses loudly and flares out a flap of skin, called the 'hood', around its neck. The snake then squeezes venom glands to spit the chemical arsenal through forward-facing holes in its fangs. The snake wiggles its head to increase the range of the spray and can even hit the eyes of moving targets.

AWESOME!

THESE SNAKES CAN SCORE A DIRECT HIT FROM A DISTANCE OF 1.5 METRES FROM THEIR ATTACKERS.

MEANWHILE, AT THE MOVIES...

SUPERHERO STYLE

COMIC-BOOK CHARACTERS AND ACTION HEROES THAT USE VENOM TO ATTACK THEIR ENEMIES INCLUDE:

POISON IVY BATMAN'S FEMALE FOE USES THE POISON FROM ANIMALS AND PLANTS TO MAKE HER BODY TOXIC TO ALL WHO TOUCH HER.

VIPER THE EVIL ADVERSARY OF THE AVENGERS AND X-MEN USES VENOM-TIPPED DARTS AND FANGS FILLED WITH POISON TO PARALYSE HER OPPONENTS.

AIM FOR THE EYES

The venom of a spitting cobra causes intense pain when it hits the eyes. The venom destroys tiny blood vessels in the eyes and leads to temporary blindness. This gives the snake a chance to escape while its attacker writhes around in absolute agony. If enough venom gets into the victim's blood, there is a very high probability of death!

THE TARSIER'S BIONIC VISION

WOW!

EACH OF THE TARSIER'S EYEBALLS IS BIGGER THAN ITS BRAIN.

The tarsiers are a group of small mammals that are closely related to the primates, which include monkeys, apes and people. These squirrel-sized creatures live in the tropical rainforests of Southeast Asia. They are nocturnal animals with absolutely enormous eyes – which give them amazing night vision.

Once common primates, today tarsiers are only found on a few islands in the Philippines in Southeast Asia. Tarsiers are arboreal (tree-dwelling) mammals and roam through the rainforest in search of food. Insects are the tarsier's favourite food, but they will also eat bats, small birds and reptiles.

SUPER NATURAL POWER!

Tarsiers have amazing eyesight. A tarsier's brain is rewired to process the information its enormous eyes receive. This processing power gives the tarsier fantastic night vision. The tarsier's eyes are fixed in their eye sockets, so the animal cannot move them around like human eyes. Instead, the tarsier moves its entire head around almost 180 degrees and uses its acute sense of hearing to pick out the movement of its prey.

AWESOME!

THE TARSIER'S SUPERNATURAL ABILITY TO SEE IN THE DARK MAKE IT A FORMIDABLE NOCTURNAL HUNTER.

TARSIERS AT RISK

A rare sight in the dense rainforest vegetation, tarsiers are shy animals. They are even more difficult to spot because there are so few of them. Almost all the remaining tarsiers living in Southeast Asia are in danger of extinction. One of the main threats is farming, which is destroying the tarsier's rainforest habitat. Attempts to save tarsiers in zoos have been unsuccessful because these animals are so secretive and shy.

MEANWHILE, AT THE MOVIES...
SUPERHERO STYLE

COMIC-BOOK CHARACTERS AND ACTION HEROES WITH SUPERNATURAL VISION INCLUDE:

SPIDER-MAN   SPIDER-MAN COMBINES THE TARSIER'S SUPERHUMAN NIGHT VISION WITH HIS SPIDER-SENSE, WHICH WARNS HIM OF IMMEDIATE DANGER.

SUPERMAN   SUPERMAN HAS SUPERHUMAN VISION AND CAN EVEN DETECT LIGHT SOURCES THAT ARE INVISIBLE TO PEOPLE, SUCH AS INFRARED AND ULTRAVIOLET LIGHT.

THE HEAT-SEEKING SUPERSONIC VAMPIRE BAT

Vampire bats are a group of three distinct blood-sucking flying mammals, including the common vampire bat, the hairy-legged vampire bat and the white-winged vampire bat. Sharing the ghoulish blood-sucking behaviour that gives them their common name, they use their amazing heat-detecting ability and supersonic hearing to find their victims.

During the day, vampire bats sleep in large groups, called colonies, in hollow trees and dark caves. The colony mainly consists of female bats and their babies, with a few resident males that control all the females in the colony.

CRITTER STATS!

Size: Up to 9cm long
Number of species: 3
Habitat: Tropical and subtropical areas

WOW!

THERE MAY BE UP TO 1,000 VAMPIRE BATS IN A SINGLE COLONY.

SUPER NATURAL POWER!

At night, vampire bats leave the colony to feed. They home in on prey such as birds, cattle and even people using their amazing heat-seeking abilities. They can detect infrared radiation, so they can pinpoint the heat from their victims to find their next meal. They have tiny 'leaf' pits on their heads to home in on their prey – the only other animals that have this supernatural ability are the heat-seeking pit vipers (see pages 32–33).

THE HUMAN FACTOR

WHEN A VAMPIRE BAT BITES, IT INJECTS A CHEMICAL CALLED AN ANTICOAGULANT INTO ITS VICTIM'S BLOODSTREAM. THIS STOPS THE BLOOD FROM CLOTTING SO THE BAT CAN DRINK FOR AS LONG AS IT NEEDS. SCIENTISTS ARE STUDYING THIS CHEMICAL TO USE IN MEDICINE. IT COULD BE USED TO IMPROVE THE BLOOD FLOW OF STROKE VICTIMS.

AWESOME!

A VAMPIRE BAT'S ANTICOAGULANT IS 20 TIMES STRONGER THAN ANY OTHER KNOWN ANTICOAGULANT.

SEEING IN SOUND

Vampire bats are even more amazing because they can also see in sound. They use this echolocation as a 'satellite-navigation' tool to find their way around. So vampire bats combine the superpowers of the pit viper with the pink river dolphin (see pages 30–31) – making them the ultimate animal superhero!

MEANWHILE, AT THE MOVIES...

SUPERHERO STYLE

COMIC-BOOK CHARACTERS AND SUPERHEROES WHO GAIN STRENGTH FROM DRINKING BLOOD INCLUDE:

BLADE BLADE IS A VAMPIRE SUPERHERO WHO DRINKS BLOOD TO GIVE HIM HIS SUPERNATURAL STRENGTH AND STAMINA.

DRACULA THIS FAMOUS VAMPIRE, CREATED BY BRAM STOKER, GIVES HIS NAME TO DRACULIN, THE ANTICOAGULANT PRODUCED BY VAMPIRE BATS.

THE WOOD FROG: A CRYOGENIC 'MR FREEZE'

AWESOME!

A WOOD FROG WILL EAT ANYTHING IT CAN FIT IN ITS MOUTH!

The wood frog is a North American amphibian found from Alaska east to Newfoundland. These hardy frogs live in a wide range of habitats, from mountain forests to peat bogs. Wood frogs possess the supernatural ability to survive very cold temperatures. Their bodies literally freeze in the winter and thaw out when spring returns.

Wood frogs vary in colour but are similar in size – up to 7cm long. They eat almost anything that moves, as well as algae and other plant food. Their diet also features the eggs of other amphibians, including other wood frogs!

THE HUMAN FACTOR

SURGEONS NEED TO PRESERVE THEY ORGANS THEY USE DURING TRANSPLANT OPERATIONS. SCIENTISTS HOPE TO APPLY THE WOOD FROG'S BIONIC ANTI-FREEZE ABILITY TO HUMAN ORGANS TO MAKE TRANSPLANT SURGERY MORE SUCCESSFUL.

SUPER NATURAL POWER!

These frogs have developed a supernatural ability to survive in freezing temperatures. During the winter, they hibernate in the leaf litter. Although the blood and other body tissues freeze in the sub-zero temperatures, the wood frogs still survive. They cheat death by storing urea and glycogen in their bodies. These chemicals act as cryoprotectants, which preserve the frogs' bodies from ice damage.

MEANWHILE, AT THE MOVIES...
SUPERHERO STYLE

SOME COMIC-BOOK CHARACTERS AND SUPERHEROES WHO USE ICE AS A SUPERPOWER INCLUDE:

BLIZZARD MANIPULATES FREEZING TEMPERATURES AGAINST HIS ENEMIES TO CREATE ICE BLASTS, MISSILES AND WALLS OF ICE.

MR FREEZE A SCIENTIST WHO WEARS A SPECIAL CRYOGENIC BODY SUIT TO SURVIVE AND FIGHTS HIS ARCH-RIVAL BATMAN USING A HANDHELD FREEZE GUN.

WOW!

WOOD FROGS HAVE A DARK 'MASK' OF SKIN AROUND THEIR EYES.

CIRCLE OF LIFE

Like all amphibians, female wood frogs lay their eggs in a lake or pond after mating with the males. The eggs hatch into tadpoles and slowly develop into adult frogs. Wood frogs usually breed only once in their lives. Most return to the same pool in which they were born to complete the circle of life.

GLOSSARY

amphibian An animal that spends part of its life in the water and part on the land.

arboreal Describes an animal that lives in trees.

camouflage A tactic animals use (by changing colour or shape) to blend in with their surroundings.

crustacean A large group of animals that usually have a hard outer shell, called an exoskeleton, to protect their soft bodies.

cryoprotectant A substance that protects living tissue from being damaged when it is frozen.

echolocation Finding objects, such as prey, by sending out sound waves and listening out for the echoes.

extinction When all the individuals of one species die.

fang The hollow tooth of a venomous snake through which it injects venom to kill its prey; also the sharp canine tooth of an animal that it uses to bite its prey.

gills The organs fish and some amphibians use to breathe underwater.

habitat The natural home of an animal.

hibernate To remain inactive for a long period, usually during the winter when it is cold.

infrared radiation A form of electromagnetic radiation with wavelengths longer than visible light but shorter than radio waves.

larva The young form of some animals that undergo metamorphosis.

mammal A warm-blooded animal with fur that feeds its young with milk from the female's mammary glands.

metabolism The chemical processes that take place inside the body of an animal.

metamorphosis The gradual process of change from a young form of an animal into its adult form (such as a tadpole into a frog).

nocturnal Describes an animal that is active at night.

pigment The substance that gives an object its colour.

predator An animal that hunts and eats other animals.

prey An animal that is hunted and eaten by other animals.

reptile A cold-blooded animal that has scales and reproduces by laying eggs.

species A group of living things that can reproduce.

torpor When an animal becomes less active to save energy.

venom A poisonous secretion of an animal such as a snake, which is usually delivered by a bite.

vertebrate An animal with a backbone.

FURTHER INFORMATION

BOOKS TO READ

Extraordinary Animals, Leon Gray, Wayland, 2013

Amazing Animal Senses, John Townsend, Raintree, 2013

Animal Superpowers, Christopher Hernandez, Scholastic, 2012

Awesome Animals, Belinda Gallagher, Miles Kelly Publishing Ltd, 2012

WEBSITES TO VISIT

http://natgeotv.com/uk/animal-superpowers
The National Geographic video channel has some cool video clips about animal superpowers. Discover how to catch an electric eel and find out how some snakes see the body heat of their prey.

http://www.nydailynews.com/life-style/super-natural-animals-amazing-powers-gallery-1.16667
The New York Daily News presents a gallery of animals with supernatural powers, from the colour-changing chameleon to the shape-shifting octopus.

PLACES TO GO

The Natural History Museum
Cromwell Road, London SW7 5BD
http://www.nhm.ac.uk

National Museum Cardiff
Cathays Park, Cardiff, CF10 3NP
http://www.museumwales.ac.uk/en/home/

National Museum of Scotland
Chambers Street, Edinburgh, EH1 1JF
http://www.nms.ac.uk

INDEX

PUFFERFISH,
PAGE 34

HERMIT CRAB,
PAGE 22

25/10/14